Ecosystems

Mountains

Erinn Banting

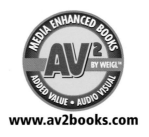

www.av2books.com

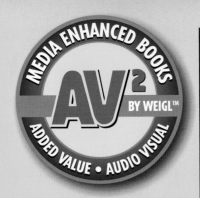

AV² provides enriched content that supplements and complements this book. Weigl's AV² books strive to create inspired learning and engage young minds in a total learning experience.

Your AV² Media Enhanced books come alive with...

Audio
Listen to sections of the book read aloud.

Key Words
Study vocabulary, and complete a matching word activity.

Video
Watch informative video clips.

Quizzes
Test your knowledge.

Go to www.av2books.com, and enter this book's unique code.

Embedded Weblinks
Gain additional information for research.

Slide Show
View images and captions, and prepare a presentation.

BOOK CODE

K365485

Try This!
Complete activities and hands-on experiments.

... and much, much more!

AV² by Weigl brings you media enhanced books that support active learning.

Published by AV² by Weigl
350 5th Avenue, 59th Floor
New York, NY 10118
Website: www.av2books.com   www.weigl.com

Library of Congress Cataloguing in Publication Data

Banting, Erinn.
  Mountains / Erinn Banting.
     p. cm. -- (Ecosystems)
  Includes index.
  ISBN 978-1-61913-073-9 (hard cover : alk. paper) -- ISBN 978-1-61913-236-8 (soft cover : alk. paper)
  1. Mountains--Juvenile literature. I. Title.
  GB512.B36 2013
  551.43'2--dc23
                    2011044151

Printed in the United States of America in North Mankato, Minnesota
1 2 3 4 5 6 7 8 9 16 15 14 13 12

012012
WEP060112

Project Coordinator Aaron Carr
Design Sonja Vogel

Every reasonable effort has been made to trace ownership and to obtain permission to reprint copyright material. The publishers would be pleased to have any errors or omissions brought to their attention so that they may be corrected in subsequent printings.

Photo Credits
Weigl acknowledges Getty Images as its primary photo supplier for this title.

Contents

What is a Mountain Ecosystem?

Mountain rivers carry tiny pieces of crushed rock downstream. This makes them lighter in color than clear water.

Earth is home to millions of different **organisms**, all of which have specific survival needs. These organisms rely on their environment, or the place where they live, for their survival. All plants and animals have relationships with their environment. They interact with the environment itself, as well as the other plants and animals within the environment. These interactions create **ecosystems**.

Mountains are a type of ecosystem. Found in a wide range of climates and regions across the globe, mountains vary a great deal. Some are tall and rocky with icy peaks, while others are low, rounded, and covered in grassy meadows. Regardless of their height or location, mountains support many unique plants and animals.

Mountains are home to some very hardy organisms. They have **adapted** to the thin air, barren soil, and freezing temperatures found at high **altitudes**. Other **species** live in the more temperate areas found at the base of mountains.

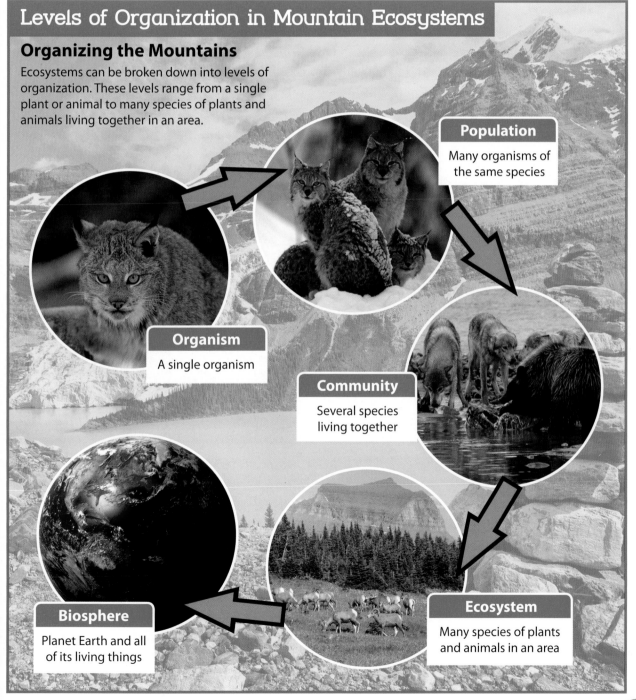

Levels of Organization in Mountain Ecosystems

Organizing the Mountains

Ecosystems can be broken down into levels of organization. These levels range from a single plant or animal to many species of plants and animals living together in an area.

Population
Many organisms of the same species

Organism
A single organism

Community
Several species living together

Ecosystem
Many species of plants and animals in an area

Biosphere
Planet Earth and all of its living things

Where in the World?

The highest point in Europe is Monte Rosa, in the Swiss Alps. Its highest peak stands 15,203 feet (4,634 m) above sea level.

Mountain ranges can be found on each of the Earth's seven continents—North America, South America, Europe, Asia, Africa, Antarctica, and Australia. Mountains are any area of land that rises 2,000 feet (610 meters) above sea level. Hills, valleys, plains, and lowlands can be found below mountains.

Mount Everest, the world's tallest peak, looms 29,035 feet (8,850 m) above sea level. Fourteen of Earth's tallest peaks, including Mount Everest, are located in the Himalayas, a mountain range in southern Asia. The Himalayas stretch from the Indus River in northern India to the Brahmaputra River in eastern India.

American Mountains

The tallest peak in North America is Mount McKinley, in Alaska. This frozen peak soars to a height of 20,320 feet (6,194 m). It is part of the Denali mountain range and was named in 1896 after William McKinley, president of the United States from 1897 to 1901.

Mountains in the Deep

Mountains are not only found on land. They can also be found deep underwater. The Mid-Atlantic Ridge runs from the Arctic Ocean to the southern tip of Africa. This arc-shaped ridge is 10,000 miles (16,000 kilometers) long. It is part of a series of sunken mountain ridges, which stretch for more than 25,000 miles (40,234 km) beneath all the world's oceans.

Eco Facts

Mountains found beneath the sea can be just as imposing as mountains on land. Some consider the island of Mauna Kea in Hawai'i to be the world's tallest mountain, since it stands more than 33,000 feet (10,000 m) off the sea floor. This is about 4,000 feet (1219 m) taller than Mount Everest.

The Himalayas have more accumulated snow and ice than any other non-polar region in the world.

Mapping the Mountains

Mountain ecosystems are found on all of the world's continents. This map shows where the world's major mountains and mountain ranges are located. Find the place where you live on the map. Do you live close to mountains? If not, which ranges are closest to you?

Legend

Mountains

Ocean Ridge

Ocean

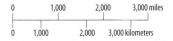 River

Scale at Equator

0   1,000   2,000   3,000 miles

0   1,000   2,000   3,000 kilometers

N

Rocky Mountains

Location: North America (United States and Canada)
Length: 3,000 miles (4,830 km)
Fact: Many rivers begin their seaward journey in the Rocky Mountains. These rivers will eventually drain into the Atlantic, Arctic, and Pacific Oceans.

Appalachian Mountains,
United States and Canada

NORTH AMERICA

Cascade Range,
United States and Canada

ATLANTIC OCEAN

Mauna Kea,
United States

Sierra Madre,
Mexico

EQUATOR

PACIFIC OCEAN

SOUTH AMERICA

East Pacific Rise,
Pacific Ocean

Andes

Location: South America (Argentina, Bolivia, Chile, Colombia, Ecuador, Peru, and Venezuela)
Length: 5,500 miles (8,851 km)
Fact: The Andes are the longest mountain range on land. The mountains of the Andes contain lush, tropical forests and frozen, high-altitude deserts.

SOUTHER OCEAN

ARCTIC OCEAN

Mid-Atlantic Ridge,
Atlantic Ocean

Himalayas

Location: Asia (Afghanistan, Bhutan, India, Myanmar, Nepal, Pakistan, and Tibet)
Length: 1,550 miles (2,500 km)
Fact: The Himalayas are one of the world's youngest mountain chains. This means that they are also the tallest, since they have experienced less **erosion.**

Carpathian Mountains,
Czech Republic, Hungary, Poland, Romania, Serbia, Slovakia, Ukraine

EUROPE

ASIA

Ural Mountains,
Russia and Kazakhstan

Altai Mountains,
China, Kazakhstan, Mongolia, Russia

Mount Kilimanjaro,
Tanzania

AFRICA

Hindukush Mountains,
Afghanistan and Pakistan

INDIAN OCEAN

PACIFIC OCEAN

Alps

Location: Western and Central Europe
Length: 750 miles (1,200 km)
Fact: The Alps are some of the most skied, hiked, and climbed mountains in the world. They are also home to some of the world's largest accessible caves.

AUSTRALIA

Southern Alps,
New Zealand

Great Dividing Range

Location: Australia
Length: 2,300 miles (3,700 km)
Fact: The mountains of the Great Dividing Range are older than almost any others on Earth. In fact, nestled in their valleys are some species of trees that have existed in their present form since Australia was connected to Antarctica, more than 80 million years ago.

ANTARCTICA

Mountain Climates

Over thousands of years, glaciers trap particles and gases from the atmosphere. From these samples, researchers can learn a great deal about the history of Earth's climate.

Mountain climates range widely, depending on the mountain's location and its height. The peaks of the tallest mountains are frozen and windy year-round. Farther below, in the valleys and at the bases of mighty mountains, temperatures are more moderate. There, snow and ice usually give way to rolling grasslands and fertile forests.

High and Cold

Temperatures drop at higher altitudes because the air thins and cannot hold the same amount of heat. There is a drop of 9 °Fahrenheit (5 °Celsius) for every elevation of 1,000 feet (305 m) on a mountain. At the lower regions of the Himalayas, temperatures average 86°F (30°C) in summer and 64°F (18°C) in winter. Higher up, however, temperatures remain below freezing throughout the year, with permanent snow and ice coverage. Even mountains close to the **equator**, such as Mount Kilimanjaro in East Africa, are covered in snow and ice year-round.

Altitude

At higher altitudes, weather becomes more violent and unpredictable. The higher a mountain is, the more wind, rain, and snow it is exposed to. Winds on Mount Everest can reach speeds of 177 miles (285 km) per hour. In the Himalayas, it is not uncommon for sudden snowstorms to drop up to 10 feet (3 m) of snow.

Eco Facts

High altitudes not only affect weather, they also affect air quality. Due to the lack of oxygen at high altitudes, people can become ill with acute mountain sickness. Symptoms of this illness include headaches, dizziness, and nausea.

Erosion

Erosion is the process of land being worn away by wind, rain, or water. Most mountains are exposed to a great deal of erosion. With no shelter from trees at higher altitudes, rock formations are worn away and chipped by wind and rain. Larger pieces of rock break into smaller boulders. Boulders become rocks. These rocks are carried down mountainsides by water and gravity.

Rain Shadows

The side of a mountain facing a coastline is called the windward side. The windward sides of mountains receive a great deal of rainfall. By the time the ocean wind reaches the opposite side of the mountain range, it has lost most of its moisture. This effect is called a rain shadow. Australia's Great Dividing Range is one example of a mountain range that causes a rain shadow. To the west of the range, where little or no rain falls for large parts of the year, the land is a desert.

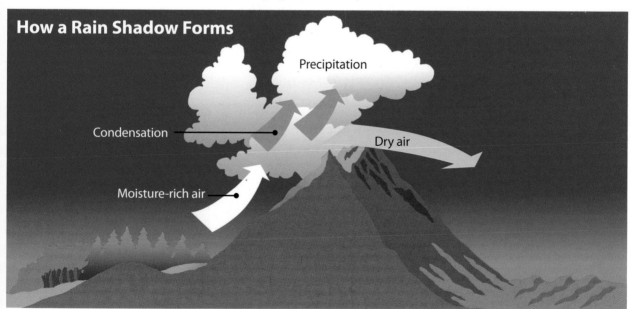

How a Rain Shadow Forms

Precipitation

Condensation

Dry air

Moisture-rich air

As air rises to cross mountains, it condenses and drops rain on the windward slopes. The dry air coming down the far side causes a rain shadow.

Types of Mountains

The Andes contain more than 30,000 species of plants and thousands of species of animals.

Earth has three layers. The crust, which can be as much as 62 miles (100 km) thick, blankets the surface. Beneath the crust is a layer of **magma** called the mantle and a core of solid iron. The crust is made up of several giant plates of rock floating on the liquid magma. Heat from Earth's core causes the magma in the mantle to flow. Over millions of years, this flow causes the plates of the crust to shift. This shifting can cause mountains to rise at the seams where the plates join. These seams are called faults.

Fold Mountains

Scientists estimate that Earth's plates move only 4 inches (10 centimeters) each year. They slowly and constantly move toward and away from each other. When two plates push against one another, layers of rock in the plates are lifted and squeezed into arches or folds. The tops of the folds become mountains.

Fault-Block Mountains

The faults between the crust's plates do not always meet smoothly. If two plates are being pushed together at a fault, one side can slide over the other, forming a mountain. The mountains of the Sierra Nevada are an example of fault-block mountains.

Dome Mountains

Dome mountains form because of the movement of magma within Earth's mantle. As magma is heated by Earth's core, it moves toward the surface. When this magma cannot escape to the surface, it creates a bubble, called a dome, in Earth's crust. The Adirondack Mountains in New York are dome mountains.

Many mountains continue to grow today. The Himalayas rise at least 1 inch (2.5 cm) each year.

Mountain Features

ountains vary greatly in location and appearance, but they share some common physical features and habitats.

Valleys

The low-lying areas between mountains are called valleys. Valleys are typically home to forests, where trees can grow, providing food and habitat for many animals. Trees will grow up the sides of mountains until they reach what is called the tree line. Above the tree line, the air is too cold, and the winds are too harsh for trees to grow.

Slopes

Vegetation can still be found above the tree line. High up on the sides of mountains, small plants grow close to the ground to shelter from the wind. Wildflowers, grasses, shrubs, and lichens make up a carpet of life known as an alpine meadow. Meadows provide food for the many birds, insects, and hardy mammals that can make the climb, such as mountain goats and llamas.

Peaks

Past certain altitudes, thin air, freezing temperatures, and harsh winds prevent any plants from growing. The peaks of the tallest mountains are always frozen and hostile to life.

Glaciers and Rivers

Rain and snow falling high in the mountains must flow somewhere. Some of it collects in packs of snow and ice called glaciers. Parts of glaciers are always melting, feeding rivers, lakes, and waterfalls further down the mountainside. These waterways form important habitats for many animals.

A great variety of animals inhabit mountain ecosystems. The large variations in altitude, temperature, weather patterns, and location allow mountains to provide homes to a vast array of organisms. These plants and animals depend on each other for the food, or energy, they need to survive. This energy transfers from one organism to another through interactions known as food webs.

Producers

The plants found in mountainous regions act as producers for other organisms in the ecosystem. These organisms are called producers because they make their own food. They also serve as food for other organisms. Producers absorb energy from the Sun and convert it into usable forms of energy, such as sugar. They make this energy through a process called **photosynthesis**. Producers found in mountains include **deciduous** and **coniferous** trees, grasses, and wildflowers.

Primary Consumers

The insects and animals that rely on producers as a food source are called primary consumers. When a primary consumer feeds on a producer, the energy made by the producer is transferred to the consumer. Examples of primary consumers found in mountain ecosystems include mammals, such as mice, caribou, and llamas, as well as seed-eating birds such as the Pine Siskin. Insects, including grasshoppers, can also be primary consumers.

Mountain Energy Pyramid

The transfer of energy in an ecosystem begins with producers and moves up the energy pyramid to the tertiary consumers. Organisms at each level of the pyramid receive energy from the organisms in the level below them.

Outside of the pyramid are the decomposers. They break down the dead and decaying **organic** matter left behind when plants and animals die. For this reason, decomposers receive energy from organisms in all levels of the energy pyramid.

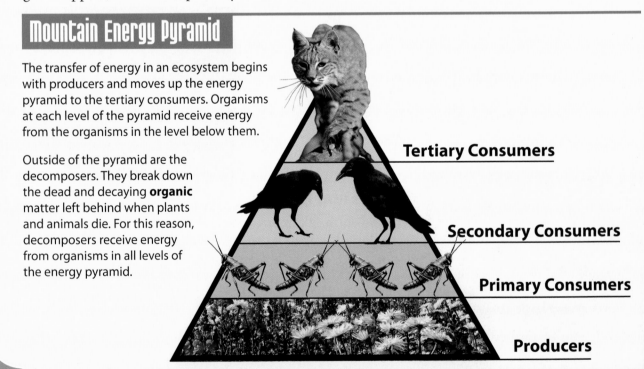

Tertiary Consumers

Secondary Consumers

Primary Consumers

Producers

Mountain Food Web

Another way to study the flow of energy through an ecosystem is by examining food chains and food webs. A food chain shows how a producer feeds a primary consumer, which then feeds a secondary consumer, and so on. However, most organisms feed on many different food sources. This practice causes food chains to interconnect, creating a food web.

In this example, the **red line** from the grass to the deer and cougar represents one food chain. The **blue line** from the conifer to the porcupine and gray wolf forms another food chain. These food chains connect in several places. The deer also feeds from conifers, and the cougar also eats porcupines. This series of connections forms a complex food web.

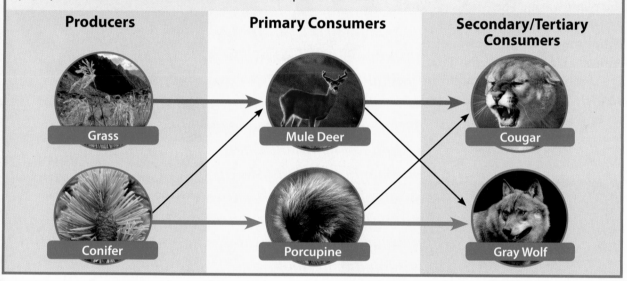

Producers	Primary Consumers	Secondary/Tertiary Consumers
Grass	Mule Deer	Cougar
Conifer	Porcupine	Gray Wolf

Secondary and Tertiary Consumers

Secondary consumers feed on both producers and primary consumers. In mountainous regions, secondary consumers include birds and reptiles, such as ravens and snakes. Spiders, dragonflies, and the fish that live in mountain rivers and lakes are also secondary consumers. Larger carnivores, such as foxes, bears, and cougars, are called tertiary consumers. Tertiary consumers feed on secondary consumers.

Decomposers

Fungi, such as mushrooms, and many types of bacteria live in mountain ecosystems. These organisms are called decomposers because they eat dead and decaying organic materials. Decomposers speed up the process of breaking down dead organic materials and releasing their **nutrients** into the soil. These nutrients are then absorbed by the roots of trees and other plants.

Plants

Wildflowers

The Alps, which stretch across western Europe, are famous for their beautiful wildflowers. Edelweiss, bluebells, campion, primroses, and buttercups are just some of the flowers that dot the lower slopes and valleys in this mountain range. Edelweiss look like small white stars. The leaves around them are furry to help keep the plant warm. The Andes of South America are home to a flower called chuquiragua, or the Flower of the Andes. Like edelweiss, the chuquiragua is a symbol of the mountains in which it resides. It is used as an herbal tea to soothe an upset stomach.

Edelweiss flowers are an important symbol in the countries surrounding the Alps. The flower's image can be seen on coins and bills, and even in the insignia of military and sporting uniforms.

Trees

Eucalyptus trees can grow to be 300 feet (91 m) tall. This makes them the tallest trees on the planet. They are native to Australia, Tasmania, and New Zealand, where they often grow on the lower slopes of mountains. The ponderosa pine grows in the Rocky Mountains of North America. It has the longest needle of any coniferous tree growing in the Rockies. When the wind blows through its needles, the ponderosa pine emits a musical sound, much like a sigh. The natural scent of this pine is similar to butterscotch.

Eucalyptus are one of the world's fastest-growing hardwood trees.

Eco Facts

Lichens are hardy organisms that share some characteristics of plants and fungi. They are able to grow in some of the most extreme environments on Earth, including mountains, at altitudes high above what other plants can tolerate.

Unique Plants

Due to their height and treacherous terrain, mountains are remote and receive little disturbance from humans. This allows some of the most unique plant life in the world to grow. The Andes are home to one curious type of plant called the Andean puya. Many people mistake it for a tree because it grows to a height of more than 30 feet (9 m). Andean puya can grow for more than 100 years before blooming thousands of brilliantly colored flowers. After it blooms, the puya dies.

Like the Andean puya, the Hawai'ian silversword only blooms once before it dies. This plant can take between 10 and 50 years to mature. It can reach a height of 6 feet (1.8 m).

Mammals

Adapting to the Mountains

Like the plants, trees, insects, and birds that call mountain regions home, mammals have found ways to adapt to different mountain conditions. Some animals, such as yaks, snow leopards, and mountain goats, have thick fur to keep them warm at tall heights. Other animals, including several species of mountain goat, nimbly climb steep slopes in search of shelter and food. Mountain goats have thick, pointed hooves to help them climb the rocky landscapes. Some animals do not live in one particular region year-round. It is common for mountain animals to move to lower slopes or warmer regions in winter.

Mountain goats require minerals in their diet to remain healthy. They sometimes go to great lengths to find salt.

Like most monkeys, Japanese macaques groom one another to remove insects that may be nesting in their fur.

Mountain Monkeys

Monkeys are well suited to life in the mountains. They use their long tails and nimble hands and feet to climb trees that line the fertile slopes. In East Africa, small vervet monkeys live in forests at altitudes of up to 13,000 feet (3,962 m). In Kyoto, Japan, there is an area called Monkey Mountain. It gets its name because of the thousands of Japanese macaques that call the slope home. Scientists recently discovered a new species of monkey in the Rungwey Mountains of Tanzania. The highland mangabey lives high in the mountains at altitudes of up to 8,000 feet (2,438 m).

Big Cats

Cougars and snow leopards are large species of cat that hunt and climb in the mountains. Unlike other large cats, snow leopards never roar. They quietly sneak up on their **prey**, such as marmots and sheep, with their large, padded paws. Cougars have incredible eyesight and can move at lightning speed. They can jump up to 18 feet (5.5 m) in the air and 40 feet (12.2 m) across the ground. Male cougars weigh an average of 136 pounds (62 kg). Most are brown, but red, gray, and black mountain lions have been found.

Eco Facts

Many bears, including the black, grizzly, and Kodiak bears found in North America's mountainous regions, survive the colder months of the year by **hibernating**.

Snow leopards have wide paws for their size. This spreads their weight and allows them to walk on deep snow without sinking into it.

Birds and Insects

Eagles and Condors

Many large birds make their home in the mountains. Mountains provide these birds with the wide open spaces their size demands, and the many ridges and shelves found on mountains are ideal for shelter and nesting. Golden eagles are found in mountainous regions all over the northern **hemisphere**. They can fly at speeds of up to 200 miles (322 km) per hour. They need to be fast to catch their quick prey, such as rabbits and hares, which dart in and out of shelter in the mountains. Andean and California condors are two of the largest species of birds found in mountain regions. The California condor weighs an average of 22 pounds (10 kg). That is the same weight as a one-year-old baby.

Golden eagles have been known to attack prey as large as deer.

The Kiwi and the Kakapo

The kiwi and kakapo are two of the most unique species of bird in the world and can only be found in the Cook Mountains of New Zealand. One reason these birds are found nowhere else in the world is because their mountain home is on an island that was separated from the mainland more than 100 million years ago. Neither species of bird can fly, and both are protected because they are **endangered** species.

Kiwis have adapted to hunt for insects on the forest floor.

Mountain Insects

In mountain ranges where temperatures are moderate, insects hop and fly through forests, valleys, and slopes. The Rocky Mountains are home to many species, including grasshoppers and ants.

Flying insects, such as the Bogong moth in Australia's Bogong Mountains, live in sheltered caves during the heat of summer. In the cooler weather of autumn, they lay their eggs. In the Himalayas, snow insects, including snow fleas and snowflies, have adapted to their frozen surroundings. These insects live in the ice and snow and survive by eating insects that are carried up the mountain by other creatures or blown there by the wind.

Soldier beetles can be found in North American mountain ranges. Gardeners often use them to control pests, such as aphids.

Mountains in Danger

Scientists continually look for ways to preserve and protect Earth's ecosystems. One of the greatest dangers faced by mountains is global warming. Global warming is the result of **greenhouse gases** in Earth's atmosphere. These gases trap the Sun's heat, which raises the temperature across the planet. Over the last 100 years, Earth's atmosphere has risen about 1.8°F (1°C). Increasing temperatures have impacted mountains around the world, causing the glaciers and snow on their summits to melt. In turn, this increases water levels in the oceans, and reduces the amount of water available to mountain ecosystems in summer.

Humans also have a negative effect on mountain ecosystems. Logging depletes forests and damages the fragile soil on rocky terrain. Mining damages mountain ranges by diverting rivers and disrupting habitats. Mining can also weaken mountains, causing dangerous avalanches and mudslides, which often destroy natural habitats and homes.

Development has also threatened mountain ecosystems. Travel through the mountains is often difficult, so railways and roads have been built in many ranges to help people pass. Unfortunately, building transportation routes has destroyed natural environments, and the pollution from vehicles is damaging to the plants and animals that live near them.

Timeline of Human Activity in Mountains

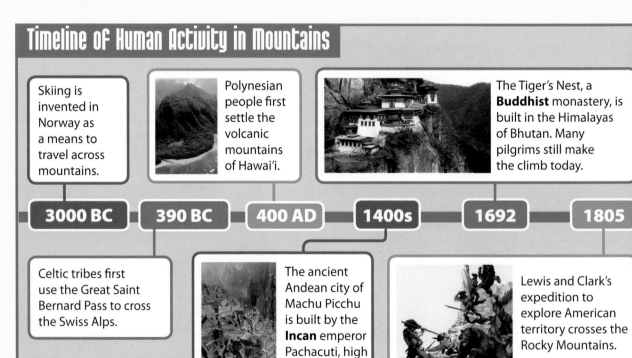

Skiing is invented in Norway as a means to travel across mountains.

Polynesian people first settle the volcanic mountains of Hawai'i.

The Tiger's Nest, a **Buddhist** monastery, is built in the Himalayas of Bhutan. Many pilgrims still make the climb today.

| 3000 BC | 390 BC | 400 AD | 1400s | 1692 | 1805 |

Celtic tribes first use the Great Saint Bernard Pass to cross the Swiss Alps.

The ancient Andean city of Machu Picchu is built by the **Incan** emperor Pachacuti, high in the Andes.

Lewis and Clark's expedition to explore American territory crosses the Rocky Mountains.

| Large-scale logging operations threaten the plants and animals that live in mountain ecosystems. |

The world's first transcontinental railroad is completed between Omaha and Sacramento, linking America across the Rocky Mountains.

The first Winter Olympic Games are held in Chamonix, France. Athletes compete in alpine events, such as skiing and bobsledding, among others.

The world's longest mountain tunnel, the Gotthard Tunnel, is scheduled to open between Milan, Italy, and Zurich, Switzerland. It is expected to be 35.4 miles (57 km) long.

1869   **1920s**   **1924**   **1953**   **1994**   **2016-2017**

Gunnar Save-Soderbergh discovers fossils of Icthyostega, one of the earliest land **vertebrates**, on a mountain in Greenland.

Sir Edmund Hillary of New Zealand becomes the first mountain climber to reach the summit of Mount Everest.

The Sustainable Forestry Initiative is launched, creating a set of environmentally friendly standards for the logging industry.

Science in the Mountains

Scientists and technicians use very precise tools to measure and record the shapes of mountains.

The study of mountains is important for scientists because mountains support a wide range of habitats. Few other ecosystems contain the same diversity of life and physical formations. Mountains, and the people who live there, help scientists learn about the history of the planet and predict its health in the future.

Digging Rocks

Mountains are composed of rock, **sediment**, and soil. Geologists study the rock composition of a mountain in order to understand how mountains form and change. To study rock composition, geologists use both simple tools and advanced equipment. This may include a hammer, compass, and notebook. More advanced tools, such as global positioning systems (GPS) may also be used. A GPS is a satellite system that measures and marks different locations.

Moving Mountains

Some geologists also study mountain movements to learn more about earthquakes and volcanic eruptions, including how to predict these events. They use seismographs, which are machines that measure the movement of Earth's plates to help predict and detect earthquake activity.

Eco Facts

Fossils of creatures normally found in the ocean have been discovered on the peaks of the Himalayas. With this evidence, scientists can prove that land once on the ocean floor was pushed up to the highest point in the world.

Fossils

Mountains can provide clues about what life was like millions of years ago. Sometimes, geologists find preserved animals and plants called fossils in the rocks of a mountain. Scientists who study fossils are known as paleontologists. They use special instruments to reveal the information fossils hold. Ion-beam microscopes fire beams of energy at fossils, and record the reflections. These reflections show the fossils much larger than their real size. This allows ion-beam microscopes to see much smaller details than regular microscopes. Other instruments are used to learn the age of rocks and fossils. From this information, paleontologists learn about the land, climate, and wildlife in Earth's distant past.

The Burgess Shale in the Rocky Mountains contains fossils of some of the earliest complex organisms on Earth. The fossils date to the Cambrian period, more than 500 million years ago.

Working in the Mountains

Many mountains are made up of very old rock that has been lifted and exposed by the movement of Earth's crust. Scientists can learn much about Earth's history by studying this ancient rock.

People who study the land, plants, and animals of the mountains perform a range of activities. They study the culture and customs of the people who live in the mountains. They also predict and monitor earthquakes and volcanic eruptions. Jobs in the mountains often involve subjects such as history, **anthropology**, biology, paleontology, **volcanology**, and **ecology**.

Environmental Scientist

Duties
Studies environments and determines ways to protect them

Education
Bachelor's degree in environmental design or natural resource management

Interests
Environment, nature, conservation

Environmental scientists study the ways in which pollution and human interaction harm the environment, including mountain ecosystems. It is their goal not to stop development, but to ensure humans live responsibly with nature. Their research is used to manage forests, parks, and wildlife protection programs.

Other Mountain Jobs

Geologist
Studies rock formations and their relationship to Earth's history and development

Research Scientist
Collects and records data in mountain environments, either for their own investigations or in support of others

Forestry Manager
Ensures that logging is done in a sustainable fashion; oversees replanting of trees, maintains wildife habitats, minimizes environmental impact

Alfred Wegener

Alfred Wegener (1880–1930) received a doctorate in astronomy in 1905, but the study of weather, and predicting it, had always been his passion. Early in his career, he used kites and hot-air balloons to study the upper atmosphere. His expertise landed him a position with a team exploring Greenland's northeast coast in 1906, where he became the first to use these techniques to study polar air.

In 1911, Wegener published a book that collected the findings he made over nearly a decade of studying the atmosphere. The book became one of the standard teaching texts in his native Germany. Wegener's curiosity, however, was unsatisfied. Examining maps, he noticed that the coasts of Africa and South America shared the same curve, leading Wegener to suspect that the continents might once have been joined together. In 1912, he became the first to propose the idea that Earth's continents might move over time.

At the time, his **hypothesis** was considered outlandish. It was not until the 1950s that Wegener's ideas about the movements of the continents were supported with proper evidence, and he was recognized as a visionary. Wegener died in 1930 in Greenland, after transporting supplies to stranded researchers far from the coast. He was last seen by his friends as he departed for the coast and was lost to a storm.

Make a Topographic Map

Topographic maps are very useful for people traveling in mountain regions. They show features like ridges and valleys by displaying changes in the height of the ground.

Materials

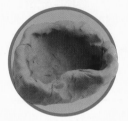

modeling clay

paper

string or fishing line

pen or marker

1. Use your modeling clay to build a small model of a mountain. Try including ridges and a peak. Be creative with the shape.

2. Wrap the string around the top of your mountain, 1 inch (2.54 cm) from the peak. Gently pull the string to slice off the top of your mountain. Repeat at 1-inch (2.54 cm) intervals until your mountain has been divided into horizontal layers.

3. Place each layer on the paper, starting with the smallest, and trace it. Be sure to keep the center of the layer in the same place each time.

Results

When you have traced each section, you will have a topographic map of your mountain. The lines on your paper show the shape of the mountain at each height. Try this activity with your friends or classmates, and have each person or team make a mountain and then a map. Then, trade maps, and put your mountains back together by stacking the layers on top of each other. See if you can use the maps to identify your friends' mountains.

Create a Food Web

Use this book, and research on the Internet, to create a food web of mountain ecosystem plants and animals. Start by finding at least three organisms of each type—producers, primary consumers, secondary consumers, and tertiary consumers. Then, begin linking these organisms together into food chains. Draw the arrows of each food chain in a different color. Use a **red** pen or crayon for one food chain and **green** and **blue** for the others. You should find that many of these food chains connect, creating a food web. Add the rest of the arrows to complete the food web using a pencil or **black** pen.

Once your food web is complete, use it to answer the following questions.

1 How would removing one organism from your food web affect the other organisms in the web?

2 What would happen to the rest of the food web if the producers were taken away?

3 How would decomposers fit into the food web?

Sample Food Web

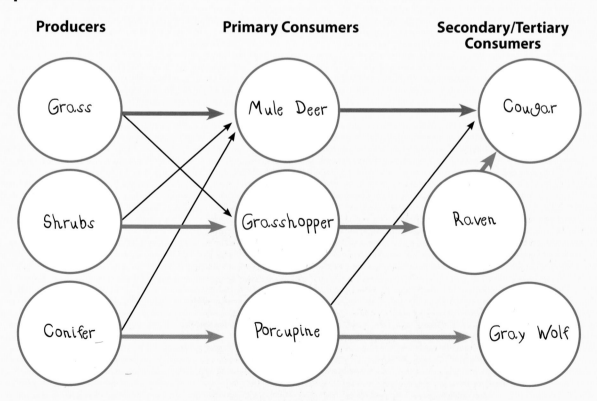

Producers	Primary Consumers	Secondary/Tertiary Consumers
Grass	Mule Deer	Cougar
Shrubs	Grasshopper	Raven
Conifer	Porcupine	Gray Wolf

Eco Challenge

1. How high above sea level must an area be to be considered a mountain?

2. On how many of Earth's continents can mountains be found?

3. Why do temperatures drop as altitude increases?

4. What is a rain shadow?

5. What are the three layers that make up Earth?

6. What type of mountain is created by pockets of magma within Earth's crust?

7. Which large cat never roars?

8. What is unique about the kiwi and kakapo birds?

9. What are some human-made threats to mountain ecosystems?

10. What do paleontologists study?

Answers

1. 2,000 feet (610 meters)
2. All seven continents
3. Thinner air cannot hold as much heat
4. An area sheltered from rain by a mountain
5. The crust, mantle, and core
6. Dome mountains
7. The snow leopard
8. Flightless, can only be found in New Zealand's Cook Mountains
9. Global warming, mining, logging, and development
10. Paleontolotists study fossils

Glossary

adapted: changed to fit the environment

altitudes: heights above sea level

anthropology: the study of human beings

Buddhist: of or relating to the religion of Buddhism

coniferous: trees that have cones and needles

deciduous: trees that shed their leaves at the end of the growing season

ecology: the study of organisms and their environments

ecosystems: communities of living things sharing an environment

endangered: in danger of becoming extinct

equator: an imaginary line drawn around Earth's center

erosion: gradual wearing away by wind and water

greenhouse gases: atmospheric gases that can reflect heat back to Earth

hemisphere: one of two halves of Earth

hibernating: passing winter in a resting state

hypothesis: a scientific guess based on limited information, meant to be a starting point for further investigation

Incan: of or relating to the Incas, a group of people living in Peru in the 13th century

magma: molten rock beneath Earth's surface

nutrients: substances essential for life and growth

organic: materials that come from living things

organisms: living things

photosynthesis: the process in which a green plant uses sunlight to change water and carbon dioxide into food for itself

prey: an animal hunted by another as food

sediment: the matter that settles to the bottom of a liquid

species: a group of similar plants and animals that can mate together and produce offspring

vertebrates: animals that have a backbone

volcanology: the study of volcanoes

Index

Log on to www.av2books.com

AV² by Weigl brings you media enhanced books that support active learning. Go to www.av2books.com, and enter the special code found on page 2 of this book. You will gain access to enriched and enhanced content that supplements and complements this book. Content includes video, audio, weblinks, quizzes, a slide show, and activities.

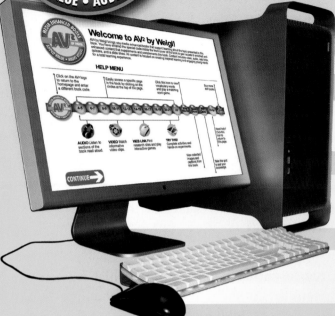

Audio
Listen to sections of the book read aloud.

Video
Watch informative video clips.

Embedded Weblinks
Gain additional information for research.

Try This!
Complete activities and hands-on experiments.

WHAT'S ONLINE?

Try This!	**Embedded Weblinks**	**Video**	**EXTRA FEATURES**
Complete an activity to test your knowledge of the levels of organization in a mountain ecosystem.	Find out more information on mountain ecosystems.	Watch a video about mountain ecosystems.	**Audio** Listen to sections of the book read aloud.
Complete an activity to test your knowledge of energy pyramids.	Learn more about the animals that live in mountain ecosystems.	Watch a video about animals that live in mountain ecosystems.	**Key Words** Study vocabulary, and complete a matching word activity.
Create a timeline of important events in mountain ecosystems.	Find out more about the plants that grow in mountain ecosystems.		**Slide Show** View images and captions, and prepare a presentation
Write a biography about a scientist.	Read about current research in mountain ecosystems.		**Quizzes** Test your knowledge.
	Learn more about threats facing mountain ecosystems.		

AV² was built to bridge the gap between print and digital. We encourage you to tell us what you like and what you want to see in the future.

Sign up to be an AV² Ambassador at www.av2books.com/ambassador.